Rookie
Read-About® Holidays

P9-DDS-657

Christmas

By Trudi Strain Trueit

Reading Consultant
Cecilia Minden-Cupp, PhD
Former Director of the Language and Literacy Program
Harvard Graduate School of Education
Cambridge, Massachusetts

Children's Press®
A Division of Scholastic Inc.
New York Toronto London Auckland Sydney
Mexico City New Delhi Hong Kong
Danbury, Connecticut

Designer: Herman Adler
Photo Researcher: Caroline Anderson
The photo on the cover shows children dragging their Christmas tree home.

Library of Congress Cataloging-in-Publication Data

Trueit, Trudi Strain.
  Christmas / by Trudi Strain Trueit.
    p. cm. — (Rookie read-about holidays)
  Includes index.
  ISBN 10: 0-531-12453-3 (lib. bdg.)   0-531-11834-7 (pbk.)
  ISBN 13: 978-0-531-12453-6 (lib. bdg.)   978-0-531-11834-4 (pbk.)
  1. Christmas—Juvenile literature. I. Title. II. Series.
  GT4985.5.T78 2007
  394.2663—dc22   2006005296

2 3 4 5 6 7 8 9 10 R 16 15 14 13 12 11 10 09   62

Twinkling lights, warm gingerbread cookies, and gifts wrapped in bright paper are some of the things that make Christmas a magical holiday.

The first Christmas was celebrated about 1,700 years ago. Christian people in Rome, Italy, chose December 25 to honor the birthday of Jesus Christ. *Christmas* means "festival of Christ."

December 2009

Sunday	Monday	Tuesday	Wednesday	Thursday	Friday	Saturday
		1	2	3	4	5
6	7	8	9	10	11	12
13	14	15	16	17	18	19
20	21	22	23	24	25	26
27	28	29	30	31		

Mistletoe

People ate, sang, and danced at early Christmas festivals. They also stood under mistletoe.

Mistletoe is a plant with white berries. Kissing someone under the mistletoe is thought to give you a long, healthy life.

People in North America started giving each other Christmas gifts in the 1800s. Children got simple presents such as fruit and candy.

Candy canes were white, straight sticks back then. Colored stripes and the hooked shape came later.

Candy canes

Santa Claus is popular in several countries.

Children hung their stockings by the fireplace for Santa Claus to fill on Christmas Eve. This tradition continues today.

In Germany, Santa Claus is known as Saint Nicholas. In Britain, children call him Father Christmas.

America borrowed many Christmas traditions from other countries. Sending Christmas cards began in England. Red poinsettia plants from Mexico are now a symbol of holiday cheer. Christmas trees got their start in Germany.

Poinsettias are a popular Christmas plant.

A modern tree decorated with lights and ornaments

14

At first, people decorated Christmas trees with paper chains, tin angels, and popcorn strings. They dyed the popcorn bright colors.

People also hung candles on trees. Strings of electric lights soon replaced the dangerous candles.

Ways to Celebrate

Christmas customs are different around the world. Children break open piñatas in Mexico. People in Finland visit the graves of their loved ones on Christmas. In many countries, people display a model of Christ's birth, called a nativity scene.

A nativity scene

Bringing a Christmas tree home

Many people in North America like to decorate a Christmas tree. Some families drive to a tree farm to cut their own tree. Others buy a living tree to plant in their yard when the holiday is over. Many people choose a fake tree.

Decorating the tree is a special event. Children in some families receive a new ornament to hang on the tree every Christmas.

Others make bread-dough ornaments. They cut them into the shapes of snowmen, angels, and wreaths.

Decorating the tree with ornaments

A gingerbread house decorated with candy

Christmas is also a time to bake goodies. You can build a gingerbread house or fill baskets with homemade cookies and bread to take to friends.

Many people attend church services on Christmas Eve. They listen to the story of Christ's birth or see it acted out as a play. Religious leaders speak about spreading peace and love. Some churches hold a candlelight service at midnight.

Children singing at a Christmas Eve service

A treat for Santa and his reindeer

Some families go caroling door-to-door on Christmas Eve. They sing popular holiday songs. Others watch their favorite holiday movie. Before children go to bed, they set out cookies and milk for Santa and carrots for his reindeer.

People open their gifts on Christmas Eve or Christmas morning. Families get up early and greet each other with "Merry Christmas!" Children rush to see what Santa left for them.

Opening presents on Christmas morning

Words You Know

candy canes

Christmas tree

church services

gingerbread house

30

mistletoe

ornaments

poinsettia

Santa Claus

Index

About the Author

Trudi Strain Trueit is a former television news reporter and weather forecaster. She has written more than thirty fiction and nonfiction books for children. Ms. Trueit lives near Seattle, Washington, with her husband Bill.

Photo Credits

Photographs © 2007: AP/Wide World Photos/Rich Abrahamson/Fort Collins Coloradoan: 25, 30 bottom left; Corbis Images/Royalty-Free: 10, 31 bottom right; Getty Images: cover (Mike Brinson/The Image Bank), 14, 30 top right (Muntz/Stone); Index Stock Imagery: 22, 30 bottom right (Derek Cole), 9, 30 top left (Wallace Garrison), 6, 31 top left (Chip Henderson), 18 (Jon Riley); Masterfile: 26 (Edward Pond), 21, 31 top right (Ariel Skelley); Superstock, Inc.: 3, 13, 17, 31 bottom left (age fotostock), 29 (Vincent Hobbs).